## PAT O'HARA

# WASHINGTON

## IMAGES OF THE LANDSCAPE

PHOTOGRAPHY BY PAT O'HARA

# WESTCLIFFE PUBLISHERS, INC.   ENGLEWOOD, COLORADO

# CONTENTS

Foreword                        9
Preface                        13
Morning Light                  14
Flora                          38
Water                          58
Daylight Interludes            78
Microcosm                      96
Coast                         112
Mountains                     126
Evening Light                 146
Technical Information         160

International Standard Book Number: ISBN 0-942394-53-4
Library of Congress Catalogue Card Number: 86-051594
Copyright, Photographs and Text: Pat O'Hara, 1987
Copyright, Foreword: Tim McNulty
Designer: Gerald Miller Simpson/Denver
Editor: Scott Lankford
Typographer: Dianne J. Borneman
Printer: Dai Nippon Printing Company, Ltd., Tokyo, Japan
Publisher: Westcliffe Publishers, Inc.
2650 South Zuni Street
Englewood, Colorado 80110

### Bibliography, John Muir Quotations

[The source is followed by the page number in this book on which the quotation appears.]

1. *The Mountains of California* (The Century Co., New York, 1894, 1911, 1912)
   "A Near View of the High Sierra": 16, 20, 60, 102.
   "A Wind-Storm in the Forest": 28, 48, 80, 86, 154.
   "The River Floods": 106.
2. *Our National Parks* (1901);
   "Wild Parks and Reservations": 30, 32, 36, 50, 52, 54, 64, 84, 92, 116, 140, 150.
   "The American Forests": 90.
3. "The Forests of Oregon," *Picturesque California* (1888): 42, 44, 46, 74, 114.
4. From *John of the Mountains: The Unpublished Journals of John Muir,* edited by Linnie Marsh Wolfe. Copyright 1938 by Wanda Muir Hanna. Copyright renewed 1966 by John Muir Hanna and Ralph Eugene Wolfe. Reprinted by permission of Houghton Mifflin Company: Foreword, 62, 100, 108, 122, 124, 138, 148.
5. From *My First Summer in the Sierra* by John Muir. Copyright 1911 by John Muir. Copyright 1916 by Houghton Mifflin Company. Copyright renewed 1939 by Wanda Muir Hanna. Reprinted by permission of Houghton Mifflin Company: 68.
6. "The Discovery of Glacier Bay," *The Century Magazine* (June, 1895): 26, 70, 76, 110, 144.
7. *Travels in Alaska* (1915): 94, 98.
8. "Twenty Hill Hollow," *Overland Monthly* (April, 1872): 118.
9. "An Ascent of Mount Rainier," from *Steep Trails* by John Muir. Copyright 1918 by Houghton Mifflin Company. Copyright renewed 1946 by Helen Muir Funk. Reprinted by permission of Houghton Mifflin Company: 128, 132, 134, 156.
10. *Son of the Wilderness* (Alfred A. Knopf, New York, 1945): 142.
11. *The Wilderness World of John Muir,* Edited by E.A. Teale (Houghton Mifflin, Boston, 1954): Foreword.

*First frontispiece: Mount Baker's snowy flanks, Mount Baker Wilderness*

*Second frontispiece: Moonrise over Point of the Arches, Olympic National Park*

*Third frontispiece: Pink monkeyflowers and scenecio create an alpine garden, Goat Rocks Wilderness*

*Title Page: Early-morning light reveals Prusik Peak's watery image in Gnome Tarn, Enchantment Basin, Alpine Lakes Wilderness*

*Right: Bracken fern and vine maple, Mount Rainier National Park*

# FOREWORD

This book represents the first comprehensive selection ever assembled from John Muir's writings on the state of Washington and the Pacific Northwest. Muir made three journeys to the Pacific Northwest: in 1879 and 1880 while en route to Alaska, and in 1888 when he scaled Mount Rainier. Best known for his writings about the wildernesses of California and Alaska, Muir was also deeply influenced by the beauty of Washington State. In fact, Muir was instrumental in the formation of Mount Rainier National Park, which was just a forest reserve when he first crossed its forests and glacier-fed streams.

Unlike his famous writings on California and Alaska, Muir's observations about Washington's wilderness were never published in book form, except as sidetrips in volumes devoted to other locations. By presenting, for the first time in a single volume focused on Washington, a careful selection from his Northwest writings, we hope to help establish John Muir as a foremost—if not the foremost—wilderness poet of the Pacific Northwest.

—Scott Lankford
Program in Modern Thought and Literature
Stanford University

Just over a century ago, in the summer of 1879, John Muir, America's best-known conservationist and naturalist, made his first visit to Washington State. Having left the open pine forests and sear grass hills of California, Muir found the lush timbered coastlines and glacier-clad peaks of the Pacific Northwest much to his liking. Of the Northwest landscape, he noted in his journal, "I never before had scenery before me so hopelessly, overabundantly beautiful for description . . . the whole is so tender, so fine, so ethereal, any penwork seems coarse and utterly unavailing."

Muir would return to Washington twice over the next two years, and complete, among other explorations, the arduous ascent of Washington's highest summit, Mount Rainier. But apart from his account of the Mount Rainier climb, few of his journal entries from this time have been published. Here, in company with the work of Pat O'Hara, one of our finest nature photographers, Muir's writing lends a poetic voice to the natural beauty of the Washington landscape.

Though separated in time by a century, the work of Pat O'Hara and John Muir share a remarkable affinity. Both men steeped themselves in the American wilderness; their lives and their work have been nourished and shaped by it. As a result, both have dedicated themselves to the preservation of our wilderness heritage—Muir, from the very dawn of wilderness awareness in our country, and O'Hara from a time when decisions are being made about the fate of our last unprotected wildlands.

Well before his death in 1914, Muir had attained prominence as America's most passionate and eloquent defender of wilderness. His legacy includes Yosemite and King's Canyon national parks in the Sierra Nevada of California, as well as Grand Canyon and Petrified Forest national parks in Arizona. By establishing the Sierra Club and serving as president during its formative years, he insured that the young preservation movement would have a permanent and powerful voice.

Muir also left his mark on the natural sciences. His name graces a list of North American fauna and flora discovered or noted during his extensive mountain travels. He was singularly responsible for the discovery of the major role played by glaciers in carving Yosemite's striking landscape, and offered to his eminent critics irrevocable proof of his findings in the form of living glaciers high in the Sierra wilderness. Muir was first to explore the Ice Age landscape of Glacier Bay in Alaska, and his natural history writings have become classics in their field.

But there was something deeper in Muir's vision. He possessed a clear and intuitive insight into the complex interactions and relationships encompassed by the mountain world. Long before Aldo Leopold introduced the concept of ecology to the general public, Muir celebrated, through his prose and through his very being, that lovely undulating wholeness that flows through all of nature, uniting the natural world and tying us irrevocably to it.

In many ways, Muir was the direct descendant of a 19th-century movement in American thought and literature known as transcendentalism. Writers such as Thoreau and Emerson (whose essays Muir took with him into the high Sierra) saw the spiritual world as manifest in nature. For them, the experience of nature was one means by which man might contact that part of his own nature which was divine. Their writings marked a major turning point in the way Americans perceived the natural world. The young Muir found in these writings a seed that he would nourish into a vision which embraced the American wilderness as a "window opening into heaven."

It was the fullness of Muir's involvement with wilderness—an involvement that engaged every part of his being—that imparted such energy to his writing. And it is this energy which ties his

*Clouds swirl above Summit Chief Mountain, Overcoat Peak, and Chimney Rock, Alpine Lakes Wilderness*

writing so closely to the contemporary photographic work of Pat O'Hara.

Though my travels with John Muir have been only through his writings, I've accompanied O'Hara on numerous trips into the mountains. Over the years, O'Hara has immersed himself in the natural landscape. As does Muir, he believes that nature deserves no less than our intimate attention—on foot, preferably, and for extended periods of time. O'Hara approaches his work with care, patience, a sure eye, and a keen sensitivity to the nuances and relationships of the natural world. His is a sensitivity much like Muir's, born of an apprenticeship of long days and quiet nights spent in wilderness—only in O'Hara's case it was the mountains, forests, rivers, and coasts of his native Washington.

Both John Muir and Pat O'Hara came to their chosen work by their own singular paths, but their paths were not unsimilar. When Muir was a young and gifted inventor working in Indianapolis, an industrial accident that resulted in temporary blindness caused him to resolve that, should his sight ever return, he would waste no more of his precious time on this earth in factories. Soon after his recovery, he left for a thousand-mile walk to the Gulf. It was this journey, and the ones that followed in the Sierra, that led to a lifetime's dedication to the preservation of wilderness.

For O'Hara, having grown up amidst the beauty of the Washington landscape, it was his experience as a young man in the war zone of Vietnam that awakened him to the preciousness of all life. This realization, coming as it did in a strife-torn landscape, led to a resolve to align his life with those parts of our world still unspoiled by the reckless hand of man. O'Hara tells of his return flight home to the Northwest, descending at dawn as the early flood of rose light washed over the winter-blue snow and ice of the Olympic Mountains. It was the same world he had grown up with, but like Muir at an infirmary window in Indianapolis a hundred years earlier, he was seeing it with new eyes.

O'Hara continued to hone his vision, with camera and lens along the Yakima River corridor while a student at Central Washington University, and later while pursuing a master's degree in forest resources at the University of Washington. This technical background lends an insight and ecological sensitivity to O'Hara's work that remains one of its distinctive hallmarks. Dramatic mountain vistas are often composed with rock and lichen—the visible process of soil formation—close up in the foreground. The distant view of an alpine glacier may be bordered with a foreground of its bouldery terminal moraine. An intimate forest floor design may juxtapose silvery decomposing wood with young and delicate blossoms of burgeoning life. Always process, always relationship. As did Muir before him, O'Hara always has an eye for the big picture. And as with Muir, his eye has made a difference. In 1984, the publication of *Washington Wilderness: The Unfinished Work*, which featured O'Hara's photography, was instrumental in helping pass legislation that secured more than a million acres of the state's finest wildlands for our National Wilderness System.

"There are moments that I wait for in photography," O'Hara once told me, "when just the right combination of factors come together: light, atmosphere, wind, feeling . . . you never know when it's going to happen so I try to remain patient and alert, mostly just open to the world before me." Late in his life, John Muir noted in his journal, "I only went out for a walk and finally concluded to stay out till sundown, for going out, I found, was really going in." For O'Hara, those crystalline moments when the world opened before him have given us some of the most stunning nature images created. In these images, the world becomes more than the sum of its elements, and its great power, mystery, and spirit seem revealed. The evening light at Point of the Arches, the sunlike clarity of mountain wildflowers in the Goat Rocks Wilderness, horses feeding in a winter pasture in the Kittitas Valley. When we view these, and so many of O'Hara's finest images, we glimpse more than the pristine beauty of the earth. We recognize something deep in our own nature, something beyond our ability to discern or quantify. We see something of the eternal.

It is my belief that John Muir and Pat O'Hara would have gotten along famously. Sharing a vision from the far corners of a century, they have allied themselves with the same timeless world. As we travel with them through the mountains, plateau lands, rivers, and coasts of Washington, let's remember to step lightly. And sip our tea slowly under the stars.

—Tim McNulty

*Comet Falls and Van Trump Creek, Mount Rainier National Park*

# PREFACE

Nature photography, for me, has required a long-term, personal commitment. My eight-year dedication has evolved into a spirited lifestyle, as well as a professional pursuit. My destiny has been shaped by love for the land, quest for creative expression, encouragement of others, hard work, and pure luck.

Wilderness is the quintessential setting for much of my image-making. I have derived inspiration from large and small nature preserves throughout the West. Washington State's abundant natural resources formed the foundation for my environmental values, as well as enriched my visual sensitivity to the landscape.

Born and reared in the Puget Sound Basin, I took for granted, at first, the natural beauty that surrounded me. Only during my post-teen years, when I left Washington for a tour in the Air Force, did I begin to realize how much the mountains and forests had influenced my being. I was homesick for the landscape.

After leaving the military, which included an obligatory migration to Vietnam, I returned to Washington and used the G.I. Bill for college. Throughout my undergraduate years, I placed a high priority on backpacking into the wilderness Northwest. My interests in nature photography and preservation of natural resources developed concurrently, nurturing and perpetuating each other.

Following graduate work in Forest Resources and a few years of various outdoor-related jobs, I made the transition into full-time photography. The subsistence stages of my new career were spent mostly in the Northwest. As time passed, I accepted more assignments out of the region, reducing the amount of time for exploring Washington.

Completion of this book on Washington State has brought me full circle. I was eager for a provincial project that would enable me to get to know my state more intimately. In some ways I feel like a "born-again Washingtonian" now that this book has taken shape.

As we enter 1987, Tina and I have had our first child. We intend to introduce our little one to nature at a very early age. We're excited to see the world in a new way through the inquisitive eyes of our daughter.

I look to the future with enthusiasm, and with hope that human kindness and environmental responsibility will prevail. Perhaps our paths will cross again in the pages of another book or in person along a wilderness trail, and I can share with you more *Images of the Landscape*, peaceful representations of a healthy world.

You hold in your hands a collection of two-dimensional imagery, but I'd like to leave you with a fond *re*collection of a three-dimensional wilderness experience.

Late in the day we hiked the gentle trail along the Soleduck River. Large Douglas fir, western hemlock, and silver fir provided an evergreen canopy to our passageway. We soon stopped to make camp for the night next to the Soleduck River crossing.

Our goal for this July backpacking trip was to reach the High Divide on the second day out. We planned to spend a couple days roaming the alpine meadows above Hoh River Valley and Seven Lakes Basin, then return via Deer Lake. This loop trip is a popular route in Olympic National Park.

We left early the next morning, ascending the trail toward Heart Lake. Dew was suspended from sedges, columbines, and tiger lilies. By mid-morning we had bypassed the lake and stood on the High Divide northwest of Cat Peak. Mount Olympus and Blue Glacier stretched across the horizon to the south. Residual fog still blanketed the Hoh River Valley below us. To the southwest, the Bailey Range formed a wall of rugged topography, including the profiles of Mount Carrie, Stephen Peak, and Mount Ferry.

We continued along the trail to the east and found an established campsite with a superb view across the Hoh River and accessibility to Seven Lakes Basin. After setting up camp, we walked along the divide past fields of wildflowers, then returned to traverse a snowfield into the basin toward an abstract patch of brilliant yellow and green. As we approached, it became clear what it was we were seeing. Moisture seeping out of the hillside had created an alpine garden of moss and yellow monkeyflowers more colorful than anything I had ever seen in the Olympics.

We spent the afternoon wandering Seven Lakes Basin, then headed back to camp for dinner and evening-light photography. The day was full and rewarding. We slept well that night.

I awoke very early the next morning to photograph the rose light of pre-dawn and the low-angle illumination after sunrise. Around 4:30 a.m. I crawled out of the tent. No sooner had I pulled on my boots than two Roosevelt bull elk walked onto the prow of a nearby hill. Their muscular bodies and huge, branching antlers were silhouetted against the rose light and outline of the Bailey Range. Steam billowed from their nostrils as they paused in the morning light. They turned their heads toward me for a moment—a brief contact and nervous acknowledgment—then bolted off downslope. I was transfixed . . . no photographs, but one of those short, intense experiences imprinted in my memory.

After the numbness of the encounter wore off, I resumed my positioning for the forthcoming sidelight. The sun crested the peaks of the Bailey Range. Lupine, avalanche lilies, and false hellebore seemed to glow from within under the delicate morning light, with Mount Olympus providing the backdrop. The scene was beautiful, but somehow anticlimactic.

Tina and I spent two more days on the High Divide. The views continued to be superb and the wildflower displays lovely. I knew my photo endeavors were successful, but not as important as the lingering memory of the silhouetted elk at pre-dawn—a poignant and gratifying preoccupation.

PAT O'HARA

*For Christina and Trisha*

---

*A distant Mount Adams and wildflower slopes, Goat Rocks Wilderness*

# MORNING LIGHT

Rose light colors the Washington State horizon around 4 a.m. at the time of summer solstice. Photography begins at this hour, as the pre-dawn light progresses from the vivid red-purples to yellowish-oranges at sunrise. The hour or so preceding sunrise is a time of exquisite light. Landforms and other natural features are starkly juxtaposed against the changing colors of the morning sky. When clouds are present, the potential exists for spectacular early-morning light shows.

In the mountains, the highest peaks catch the first direct, but soft, radiance of the morning sun. As the sun's angle swings above the horizon, the light melts down the western slope. With its diffusion relieved, it becomes more intense. The interplay of deep shadows and illuminated detail accentuates the furrowed character of the mountain landscapes. The two- to three-hour transition from rose light to sunrise to post-sunrise is priority image-making time. My visual interpretation of the landscape is often influenced by the graphic design created from form, texture, and color. All three elements are affected by light, which determines my compositional approach to elements in nature. Some of my most successful compositions have been created in morning light. During the summer months, my serious efforts are often concluded by 7 a.m., when light flattens and shadows shrink.

Winter months in Washington provide image-making opportunities later into the mornings. The days are shorter and the sun is much farther south. Thus, shadows persist and the quality of light is maintained.

Morning light is synonymous with quiet places, dew-covered meadows, cold hands, vapored breath, and warm thoughts. It is taken for granted by those who sleep.

*Mount Rainier reflects onto Reflection Lake through morning mist, Mount Rainier National Park*

Chetwoot Lake emerges from pre-dawn shadows, Alpine Lakes Wilderness

Slanting light dapples Mount Adams, viewed from the Goat Rocks Wilderness

Overleaf: Morning clouds crown Mount Stuart and Ingalls Lake,
Alpine Lakes Wilderness

"... *Then, penetrate the wilderness where you may, the main telling
features, subordinate, are quickly perceived, and the most complicated
clusters of peaks stand revealed harmoniously correlated and
fashioned like works of art—eloquent monuments of the ancient ice
rivers that brought them into relief from the general
mass of the range...*"

*Deer Park lichens frame Needles Peaks and Gray Wolf Ridge,*
*Olympic National Park*

*Dawn's light paints the Nisqually River, Nisqually National Wildlife Refuge*

"*How glorious a greeting the sun gives the mountains! To behold this alone is worth the pains of any excursion a thousand times over. The highest peaks burned like islands in a sea of liquid shade. Then the lower peaks and spires caught the glow, and long lances of light, streaming through many a notch and pass, fell thick on the frozen meadows.*"

Mount Challenger and Whatcom Peak, North Cascades National Park

Remnants of the cataclysm, crater dome's barren slopes from Smith Creek
Overlook, Mount Saint Helens National Volcanic Monument

Overleaf: Sunlight emerges through morning mist above Lake Leo,
Colville National Forest

" . . . We stood hushed and awe-stricken, gazing at the holy vision;
and had we seen the heavens open and God made manifest, our
attention could not have been more tremendously strange. When the
highest peak began to burn, it did not seem to be steeped in sunshine,
however glorious, but rather as if it had been thrust into the body of
the sun itself."

*Morning light illuminates the Summerland area, Mount Rainier National Park*

*Sun crests a cloud bank stretching from Mount Baker to Blue Mountain, Olympic National Park*

"*The sunrise we did not see at all, for we were beneath the shadows . . . but in the midst of our studies we were startled by the sudden appearance of a red light burning with a strange, unearthly splendor on the topmost peak. . . . Instead of vanishing as suddenly as it had appeared, it spread until the whole range was filled with the celestial fire. . . .*"

*Horses feed in winter fog, eastern Cascade slopes*

*Snow-sculpted trees atop Mission Ridge, Wenatchee Mountains*

"*. . . The snow bends and trims the upper forests every winter, the lightning strikes a single tree here and there, while avalanches mow down thousands at a swoop as a gardener trims out a bed of flowers. But the winds go to every tree, fingering every leaf and branch and furrowed bole; not one is forgotten; the mountain pine towering with outstretched arms on the rugged buttresses of the icy peaks, the lowliest and most retiring tenant of the dells. . .*"

Misty morning light, Yakima River

Morning frost sparkles on the shore of Nile Lake, Colville National Forest

"Most of the farm lands of Washington . . . lie on the east side of the mountains. The forests on the eastern slopes of the Cascades fall altogether ere the foot of the range is reached, stayed by drought as suddenly as on the west side they are stopped by the sea. . . ."

Moonset over the mountains, Olympic National Park

Mount Rainier pierces through clouds near Lake Louise,
Mount Rainier National Park

Overleaf: Endlessly blue horizons in Little Beaver Valley,
North Cascades National Park

" *. . .In the center of it [the Rainier region] there is a lonely mountain
capped with ice; from the ice-cap glaciers radiate in every direction,
and young rivers from the glaciers; while its flanks, sweeping down in
beautiful curves, are clad with forests and gardens. . . .*"

*Indian Henry's Hunting Ground, Mount Rainier National Park*

*Morning scene reflects on Upper Lena Lake, Olympic National Park*

"*Its [Mount Rainier's] massive white dome rises out of its forests,
like a world by itself, to a height of fourteen thousand to fifteen
thousand feet. The forests reach to a height of a little over six thousand
feet, and above the forests there is a zone of the loveliest flowers, fifty
miles in circuit and nearly two miles wide. . . .*"

# FLORA

The rhododendron is Washington's state flower. Its showy pink blooms appear along Hood Canal early in May and on into June. Although limited in geographic distribution to west of the Cascade Mountains, this species is symbolic of the wealth of flora (plant life) that forms the many distinct biotic life zones of the Evergreen State.

During spring, the sagebrush flats and hills of the Columbia River Basin transform into low-growing gardens of phlox, balsamroot, and lupine, intermixed with countless other dryland species. Surviving in the rain shadow of the Cascades, these floral displays are some of the most impressive and photogenic in the state.

Alpine meadows begin to bloom as the snow recedes about the time of summer solstice. The growing season is short but intense. Fields of glacier lilies, Indian paintbrush, and asters grace the surrounding rocky terrain.

The lush forests of the western side provide an evergreen overstory to a floor of flowers, ferns, and mosses. Douglas fir, Western hemlock, and red cedar—where protected—grow to gigantic proportions.

Autumn colors in the Kettle Range along Highway 20 in northeastern Washington are some of the most impressive in the state. Western larch, cottonwoods, aspen, and birch display their brilliant foliage in October. The area around Sherman Pass is particularly scenic.

Winter ornaments eastern Washington's riparian vegetation. Along the river corridors, frost and ice embellish red-osier dogwood, sumac, northern black cottonwoods, and ponderosa pine. The Wenatchee, Yakima, and Methow river systems draining the eastern slope of the Cascades provide excellent photographic possibilities, as well as the Pend Orielle, Sanpoil, and Palouse rivers farther east.

Flora often is a dominant element in my landscape photography. Its abundance in Washington is fortuitously unavoidable. I am often drawn to landscape compositions because of their colorful foreground flora, especially wildflowers. Some of the most beautiful gardens I have ever observed were propagated naturally in the wild.

*Striped profusion of flowering lupine, scenecio, and pink monkeyflowers, Goat Rocks Wilderness*

*Overleaf: Moss drips from vine maples, Hoh Rain Forest, Olympic National Park*

Phlox and weathered log, Glacier Peak Wilderness

Rocks paved with violet larkspur, Goat Rocks Wilderness

"Along the slopes of the Cascades, where the woods are less dense
. . . there are miles of rhododendron, making glorious outbursts of
purple bloom. . .

*Tiger lilies unfurl pollen-coated stamens, Olympic National Park*

*Canyon Creek drainage, Pasayten Wilderness*

"*And down on the prairies in rich, damp hollows the blue-flowered camasia grows in such profusion. . .*

*Deer fern fiddleheads, Alpine Lakes Wilderness*

*Falls nourish pink heather, North Cascades National Park*

" . . . *That at a little distance its dense masses appear as beautiful as blue lakes imbedded in green, flowery plains.*"

Western hemlock's new growth, Olympic National Forest

Larch tree mosaic, Kettle Range, Colville National Forest

"*Colossal spires two hundred feet in height waved like supple goldenrods chanting and bowing low as if in worship, while the whole mass of their long, tremulous foliage was kindled into one continuous blaze of white sun-fire. . . .*"

*Pink monkeyflowers, Norse Peak Wilderness*

*Wild rhododendron, Olympic National Forest*

" . . .*So closely planted and luxuriant that it seems as if Nature, glad to make an open space between woods so dense and ice so deep, were economizing the precious ground. . .*

*Crimson elderberry and horsetail, Olympic National Park*

*Stonecrop wildflowers advance upon lichen-encrusted rock,
Olympic National Park*

" . . . *Trying to see how many of her darlings she can get together in
one mountain wreath. . .*

_Wildflowers and sagebrush, Columbia River Basin_

_Scotchbroom in full bloom above Dungeness Valley, Olympic Peninsula_

_Overleaf: Lupine wildflowers on Hurricane Ridge, Olympic National Park_

" _. . . Daisies, anemones, geraniums, columbines, erythroniums, larkspurs, etc., among which we wade knee-deep and waist-deep, the bright corollas in myriads touching petal to petal._"

# WATER

No other environmental factor affects Washington State landscapes so profoundly as water in its many forms. Its abundance, or lack of it, contributes to the state's distinctive ecosystems. The Pacific maritime influence and its inextricable association with mountainous topography greatly control precipitation patterns.

The water cycle, represented by rain, snow, fog, and glaciation, contributes greatly to the landforms, plant and animal life we see today. From Pacific Coast beaches, to dense rain forests, to alpine meadows and glaciated mountain peaks, to the Columbia Basin coulees, water has sculpted contemporary landscapes.

Continental glaciation scoured the region during the Pleistocene Age, while mountain glaciers cut valleys and sharpened sawtooth ridges. Over the centuries, as the glaciers retreated, the tremendous power of run-off continued—and still continues—its erosive action.

Water, as a land-forming tool, is most powerful today during winter and spring. Excessive winter snow accumulation in the high mountains provides the sculpting prowess of glaciers. In the western lowlands, winter flooding frequently takes its toll during heavy rains; along the coast, relentless wave action gnaws away at the softer material of the headlands during winter storms. Seastacks are beautiful remnants of this tenacious hydraulic action.

Run-off from spring thaw is an annual force that turns docile streams into rushing torrents, when mist billows high from the base of waterfalls. In some locations along the Skykomish and Wenatchee rivers, the force is so great that the ground quivers nearby. Sediments are carried from the high country to lower estuaries and alluvial fans. The Continental Shelf ultimately becomes the repository of the "mountains that used to be," especially from the Columbia River system.

Water is a visual magnet, drawing our attention and beckoning us to explore further. A solitary droplet suspended from sedge embodies the same mysteries as a scenic reflection in the alpine tarn where it grows. Ethereal fog nurtures the moss of coastal forests. Glacial flour suspended in the water of high mountain lakes bends light rays and creates their beautiful turquoise color.

The water cycle, as its name implies, is continuous—no universally defined beginning or end. Our planet is a cell: life is dependent upon the health of this cycle.

It is my hope that the images in this book will not only aesthetically document the water cycle, but will help stimulate an ethic that perpetuates water quality on a global basis.

*Water and rock, Skykomish River, Cascade Mountains*

*Martha Falls through the mist above Unicorn Creek,*
*Mount Rainier National Park*

*The rhythm of waves, Point of the Arches, Olympic National Park*

"*The waterfall sang in chorus, filling the old ice fountain with its solemn roar, and seeming to increase in power as the night advanced—fit voice for such a landscape.*"

*Cultivated hillside along the Columbia River, Chelan County*

*Glacier lily after a rainstorm, Olympic Mountains*

"*So truly blind is lord man; so pathetically employed in his little jobs of town-building, church-building, bread-getting, the study of the spirits and heaven, etc., that he can see nothing of the heaven he is in.*"

*Misty descent, Palouse Falls State Park*

*Falls sidestep mossy boulders beside Chelan Lakeshore Trail,
Chelan-Sawtooth Wilderness*

*Overleaf: Icy swirls in Tapto Lakes Basin below Red Face Mountain,
North Cascades National Park*

"*Beside all these bloomers there are wonderful ferneries about the
many misty waterfalls, some of the fronds ten feet high, others the
most delicate of their tribe, the maidenhair fringing the rocks within
reach of the lightest dust of the spray, while the shading trees on the
cliffs above them, leaning over, look like eager listeners anxious to
catch every tone of the restless waters.*"

*River's fierce passage through the Olympic Mountains, Buckhorn Wilderness*

*Reflection of autumn foliage, Manastash Creek*

"No pain here, no dull empty hours, no fear of the past, no fear of the future . . . Drinking this champagne water is pure leisure, so is breathing the living air. . . ."

Ice Lakes Basin, Glacier Peak Wilderness

Shadows ford Palouse River Canyon, Palouse Falls State Park

Overleaf: Flying above the rugged peaks, North Cascades National Park

" . . . [*The* glacier] not only covering, but creating, a landscape with all the features destined to have when, in the fullness of time, the fashioning ice-sheet shall be lifted by the sun, and the land shall become warm and fruitful. The view . . . from base to summit, every peak and spire and dividing ridge of all the mighty host, was of a spotless, solid white, as if painted."

Pink monkeyflowers border a stream near Deep Lake, Alpine Lakes Wilderness

*Fluid movement in morning light, Wenatchee River*

*"Passing from beneath the shadows of the woods where the trees grow close and high, we step into charming wild gardens full of lilies, orchids, heathworts, roses, etc., with colors so gay and forming such sumptuous masses of bloom, they make the gardens of civilization, however lovingly cared for, seem pathetic and silly."*

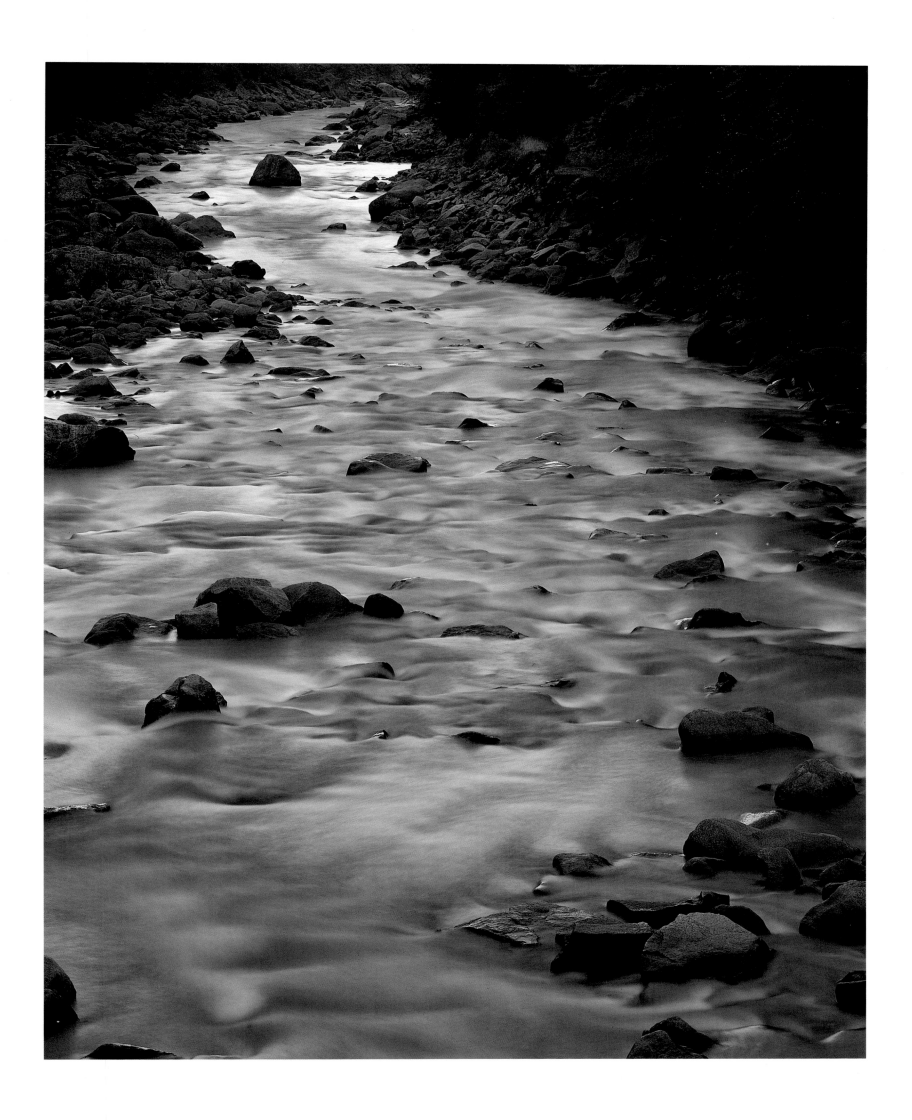

*Columbia Glacier in summer repose above Lake Blanca,*
*Henry Jackson Wilderness*

*Creek and icicles near Hurricane Ridge, Olympic National Park*

"**E**merging from its icy sepulcher, it gives a most telling illustration
of the birth of a marked feature of a landscape. In this instance it is
not the mountain, but the glacier, that is in labor, and the mountain
itself being brought forth."

# DAYLIGHT INTERLUDES

Most successful landscape images are created during early morning and evening. Dawn and sunset often provide the best lighting, when the low angle of the sun casts elongated shadows, and harsh edges soften in the diffusion.

The interlude between morning and evening is a time of changing light quality. On sunny days, light flattens during midday and photographic potential often declines. Some landscape photographers reserve this transition period for scouting purposes only.

Daylight interludes can offer alternating moments of high-quality light. This is particularly true when cloud formations are continually changing. Swirling, billowing, and shifting patterns reflect onto still water. Summer cumulus clouds build up over the mountains in mid-afternoon, creating dramatic scenes and their consequence—violent thunderstorms. Sporadic shafts of light stream through openings in the clouds to delicately touch the landscape. Rainbows can be seen any time of day as breaks occur during storms.

The interaction of sun and fog can produce striking monochromatic scenes. Winter days along the coast offer surprising moments as storm fronts pass over. At the beachfront and within the adjacent forest, color becomes secondary to form.

Overcast days present great interludes for photographing intimate landscapes without a visible horizon. Colorful hillsides, forest groves, and ground patterns are subjects whose detail is exposed with saturated clarity.

Though daylight interludes lack the special qualities of morning and evening light, they offer many fine opportunities for a variety of landscape compositions. The notion that serious image-making is exempt during the midday hours is superfluous and myopic. Visual sensitivity to the landscape is a continuous process of spontaneous response to unexpected moments, regardless of time of day.

*Pink heather flourishes against snowy backdrop of Mount Challenger and Whatcom Peak, North Cascades National Park*

Cedar tree amidst Grove of the Patriarchs, Mount Rainier National Park

Autumn landscape, Washington Park Arboretum, Seattle

Overleaf: Shelter from the snow, Kittitas Valley

"We hear much nowadays concerning the universal struggle for existence, but no struggle in the common meaning of the word was manifest here; no recognition of danger by any tree; no deprecation; but rather an invincible gladness as remote from exultation as from fear."

*Forest in fog, Olympic National Park*

*Riparian habitat, Teanaway River*

"*A*long the moist, balmy, foggy, west flank of the mountains, facing
the sea, the woods reach their highest development . . . with the giant
arbor-vitae, or cedar, and several species of fir and hemlock in varying
abundance, forming a forest kingdom unlike any other, in which limb
meets limb, touching and overlapping in bright, lively, triumphant
exuberance, two hundred and fifty, three hundred, and even four
hundred feet above the shady, mossy ground."

*View from Hurricane Ridge, Olympic National Park*

*Afternoon light glints on Scotts Creek, South Beach Wilderness,
Olympic National Park*

*Overleaf: Expanse of daffodils, Skagit Valley*

" . . . *They [winds] seek and find them all, caressing them tenderly,
bending them in lusty exercise, stimulating their growth, plucking off a
leaf or limb as required, or removing an entire tree or grove, now
whispering and cooing through the branches like a sleepy child, now
roaring like the ocean; the winds blessing the forests, the forests the
winds, with ineffable beauty and harmony as the sure result.*"

*Litter of fallen leaves, Manastash Creek*

*Maple-filtered light along Nason Creek, Cascade Mountains*

"*Any fool can destroy trees, they cannot run away; and if they could, they would still be destroyed,—chased and hunted down as long as fun or a dollar could be got out of their bark hides, branching horns, or magnificent bole backbones. Few that fell trees plant them; nor would planting avail much towards getting back anything like the noble primeval forests. . . .*"

*Western hemlock drinks in the fog, Olympic National Park*

*Sumac invades rock garden, Columbia River Basin*

" . . . *The big, gray days are exhilarating, and the colors of leaf and branch and mossy bole are then at their best. . . .*"

Dandelion seedheads canvass a farming neighborhood, Jefferson County

Autumn foliage, Colville National Forest

"*Everybody needs beauty as well as bread, places to play in and pray in where Nature may heal and cheer and give strength to body and soul alike.*"

# MICROCOSM

Grand landscapes are composites of natural detail—terrestrial fabrics interwoven with threads of living organisms and inorganic material. Although most of us are inspired by wide-angle vistas, we often overlook the minute details or individual threads that make up the visual whole. Isolation of these elements in photographic compositions is an exercise in sophisticated simplicity, or the art of seeing.

Learning to see detailed patterns and designs enables us to expand our visual awareness, our sensitivity. It frees us from ocular preconceptions and restores that refreshing sense of child-like wonder at the richness of our own backyard nature reserves. The things that we previously passed by or gave only a casual glance now may be enjoyed and appreciated.

Contrary to amateur opinion, overcast days are ideal for outdoor photography. When landscape horizons are obscured by clouds, diffused light minimizes the harsh contrasts within the microcosms, and colors are usually well-saturated. Some of the most poetic and poignant images have been composed under these conditions.

Other lighting conditions are also suitable for microcosm exploration. Strong sidelighting and backlighting affect the three-dimensional quality of compositions, each creating different chromatic presentations.

Through the photographer's eyes, visual interpretations are transferred onto film emulsion. Using different lighting conditions and other compositional techniques, a creative photographer transcends technical boundaries into the realm of image-maker—a higher level of consciousness and artistic endeavor.

*Oregon grape leaves, Olympic National Park*

Salal leaf silhouettes, Queets Rain Forest, Olympic National Park

Desert parsley sprouts from rocky outcropping, Columbia River Basin

"*The scenery of the ocean, however sublime in vast expanse, seems far less beautiful to us dry-shod animals than that of the land seen only in comparatively small patches; but when we contemplate the whole globe as one great dewdrop, striped and dotted with continents and islands, flying through space with other stars all singing and shining together as one, the whole universe appears as an infinite storm of beauty.*"

*Satin flower at sunset, Steptoe Butte State Park*

*Rime-edged bracken fern and wild rose leaves, Kettle Range*

"*If my soul could get away from this so-called prison . . . I should hover over the beauty of our own good star. I should study Nature's laws in all their crossing and unions. . . . But my first journey would be into the inner substance of flowers.*"

Water, snow, granite, Alpine Lakes Wilderness

Crystalline rain forest, Olympic National Forest

Overleaf: Alder trees at moonrise, Olympic National Park

"*All things were warming and awakening. Frozen rills began to flow . . . The lakes seen from every ridge-top were brilliantly rippled and spangled, shimmering like the thickets of the low dwarf pines. The rocks, too, seemed responsive to the vital heat—rock crystals and snow crystals trilling alike. . . .*"

*Spider web veils salal leaves, Olympic Peninsula*

*High country design, Ingalls Lakes Basin, Alpine Lakes Wilderness*

"... *The sublime whirl of planets around their suns is as silent as
raindrops oozing in the dark among the roots of plants.*"

*Thicket of red alder trees, Olympic National Park*

*Rhythms in kelp, Olympic National Park*

"*Thus it appears that everything here is marching to music, and the harmonies are all so simple and young they are easily apprehended by those who will keep still and listen and look.*"

*Autumn-dappled cottonwood leaves, Colville National Forest*

*Basalt palette, Columbia River Basin*

" . . .*From all those deadly, crushing, bitter experiences comes this delicate life and beauty, to teach us what we in our faithless ignorance and fear call destruction is creation.*"

---

*Seastars at low tide near Third Beach, South Beach Wilderness,*
*Olympic National Park*

*Mermaid's tail on Ruby Beach, Olympic National Park*

*Overleaf: Sunset from Toleak Point, South Beach Wilderness,*
*Olympic National Park*

---

" . . . *You bathe in these spirit-beams, turning round and round, as if*
*warming at a camp-fire. Presently you lose consciousness of your own*
*separate existence: you blend with the landscape, and become part*
*and parcel of nature.*"

*South Beach Wilderness, Olympic National Park*

*Play of light on beach rocks, Olympic National Park*

" . . .*G*oing out I found that I was really going in."

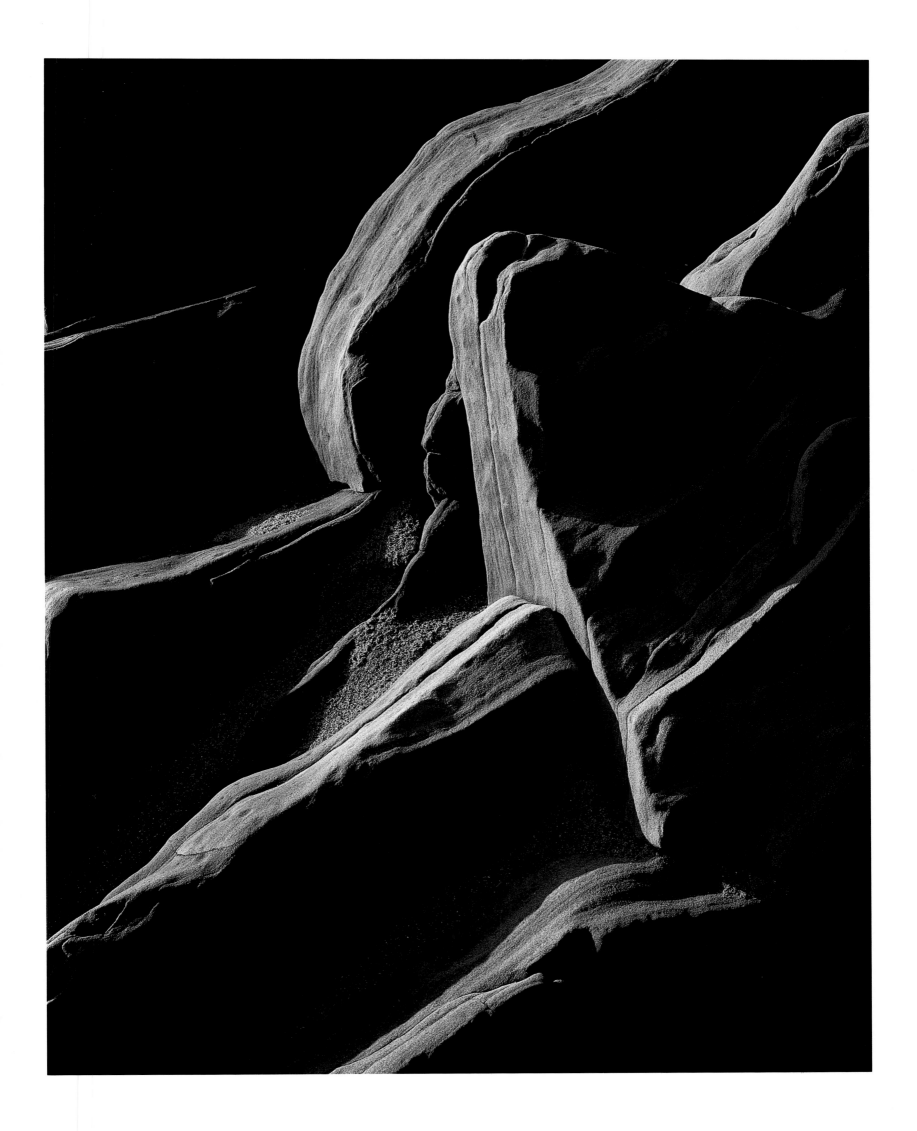

*Sunset silhouettes Point of the Arches, Olympic National Park*

*Beach pebble pathways, Olympic National Park*

"*...One feels submerged and ever seeks the free expanse....*"

# MOUNTAINS

Mount Rainier, Washington's unofficial symbol, can be seen on clear days from all corners of the state. Baker, Adams, Glacier, and Saint Helens are Rainier's smaller volcanic companions in the Washington Cascade chain.

The cataclysmic May 1980 eruption of Mount Saint Helens reminded us of the subterranean forces that so overwhelmingly affect mountain-building. The ever-present abrasion of the Pacific and Continental plates promotes this on-going thermal activity and mountain uplifting.

Mountain ranges such as the Cascades, Olympics, Kettles, Selkirks, and Blues vary in age. Each has its individual geologic beginnings and environmental influences which have created the 20th-century landscapes. Rugged peaks of the Cascades' Picket Range differ greatly from Cascade volcanic profiles. The Kettle Range has eroded down to rounded, forested hills with occasional fire-spawned meadows. The Olympics exhibit an ancient seafloor and dark formations of volcanic basalt.

Washington wilderness is characterized by pristine mountainous enclaves. These areas have survived development due to their remoteness and severe weather patterns. Public support has prompted Congress to designate vast areas of federal lands—mostly U.S. Forest Service—as part of the National Wilderness Preservation System. Three national parks—Mount Rainier, Olympic, and North Cascades—preserve special places of global significance.

Perhaps no other landscapes have had such impact on the direction of my photography. Mountains continue to be a primary source of my inspiration. The reasons are somewhat elusive; the core influences remain subliminal.

From a cognitive perspective, mountains are powerful places. Their towering supremacy is tempered, however, by delicate alpine gardens and serene lake settings. This visual symbiosis thrives in a landscape of physical incongruity.

The presence of mountains has long inspired Washington State residents, artists, and visitors. Individually and collectively, the mountains are worth saving—a gift to children of the future.

*Mount Stuart's snowy ascent from Ingalls Lake Basin,*
*Alpine Lakes Wilderness*

*Liberty Bell gilded by sunlight, North Cascades Scenic Highway*

*Little Annapurna and Rune Lake, Enchantment Basin,
Alpine Lakes Wilderness*

*Overleaf: Summit Chief Mountain, Overcoat Peak, and Chimney Rock
viewed from the Tank Lakes region, Alpine Lakes Wilderness*

"*The view we enjoyed from the summit could hardly be surpassed in
sublimity and grandeur. . .*

Autumn slopes above Lake Louise, Mount Rainier National Park

Bonanza Peak reflects in Lyman Lake, Glacier Peak Wilderness

"...*But one feels far from home so high in the sky, so much so that one is inclined to guess that, apart from the acquisition of knowledge and the exhilaration of climbing, more pleasure is to be found at the foot of mountains than on their frozen tops....*

Solitary reflection of Mount Adams broken in Takhlakh Lake,
Gifford Pinchot National Forest

Pearly everlasting springs forth from ravaged slope, Smith Creek Overlook,
Mount Saint Helens National Volcanic Monument

Overleaf: Olympic Mountains and pond reflection near Mildred Lakes,
Mount Skokomish Wilderness

" . . . Doubly happy, however, is the man to whom lofty
mountain-tops are within reach, for the lights that shine there illumine
all that lies below."

*Saxifrage wildflowers skirt boulder at the base of Mount Anderson, Olympic National Park*

*Talus boulders frame Mount Shuksan, North Cascades National Park*

"*To dine with a glacier on a sunny day is a glorious thing and makes common feasts of meat and wine ridiculous. The glacier eats hills and drinks sunbeams.*"

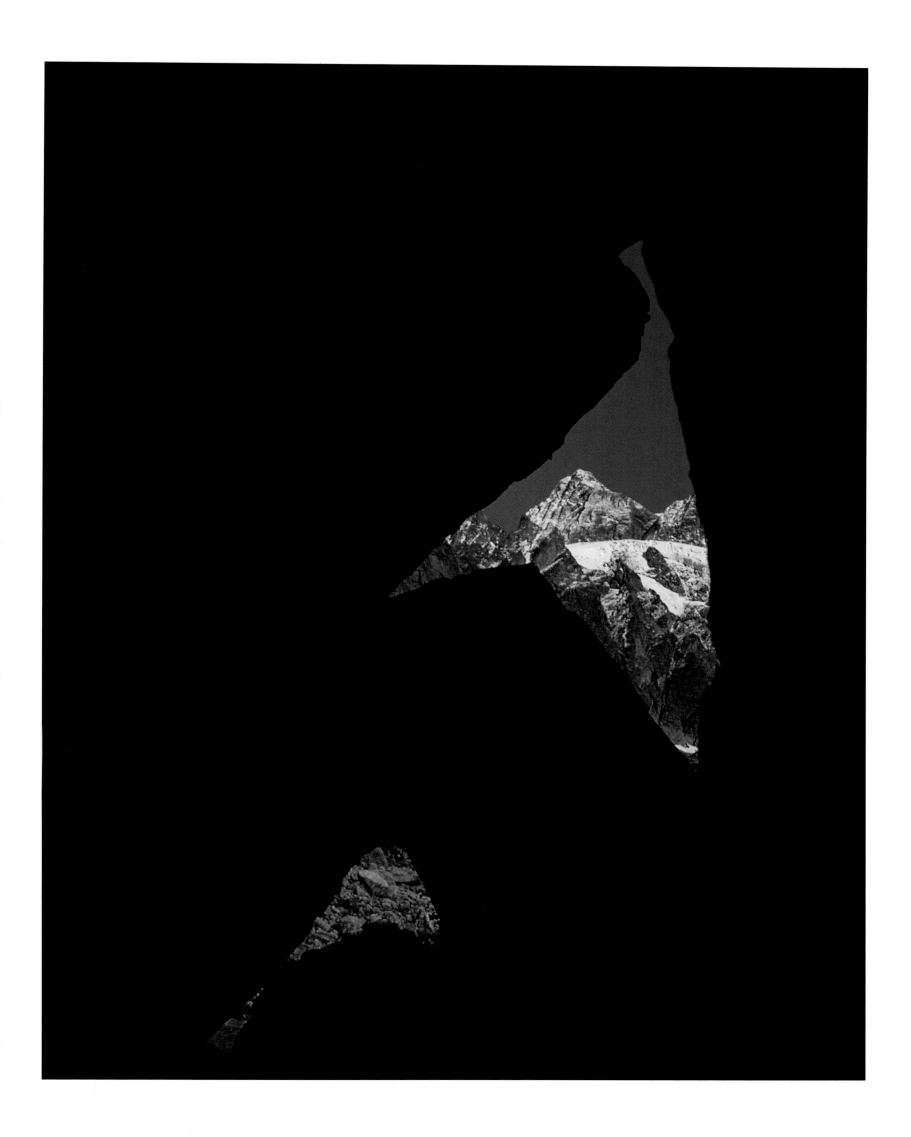

*Afternoon highlight on Mount Baker, Mount Baker Wilderness,*

*Stevens Canyon, Mount Rainier National Park*

"None of Nature's landscapes are ugly so long as they are wild; and much, we can say comfortingly, must always be in great part wild, particularly the sea and the sky, the floods of light from the stars, and the warm, unspoilable heart of the earth, infinitely beautiful, though only dimly visible to the eye of imagination."

# EVENING
# LIGHT

Evening connotes closure—the end of the day, a time for relaxation. For a serious photographer, however, it is a time of creative activity. The quality of light, of course, is the underlying motivation for this accelerated behavior.

From morning to evening, the sun arcs over the skyline. Shadows ebb, then slowly reappear like an incoming tide as evening approaches. This light-and-shadow cycle greatly affects the landscape's visual character and the way I interpret it.

When photographing in the wilderness, particularly on mountain backpacking trips, I usually scout out evening photography sites hours in advance. I try to pre-visualize how lighting conditions will affect the form, texture, and color of compositions and their exposure onto the film. I rely on experience and gut feeling to guide my judgment of lighting and camera angles. Intricate, on-site compositional adjustments are made spontaneously when image-making is in progress.

Evening light is a several-hour event comprised of pre-sunset, sunset, and post-sunset. Its quality differs slightly from morning light's because of increased levels of aerial particulates that tend to diffuse the light differently, especially on hot summer days. Deep red sunsets are usually a result of these airborne particles.

Photo opportunities continue after the sun dips over the mountains, in reverse chronology to morning light. Venus shines bright, rose light temporarily rests on the serrated ebony horizon, upper levels of the atmosphere darken, and a few faint stars become visible as a prelude to the grand appearance of the Milky Way, the galaxy which graces the vastness above.

Evening is taken for granted by those who sleep.

*Violet clouds viewed from Blue Mountain, Olympic National Park*

Moonrise and evening light on Old Snowy, Goat Rocks Wilderness

Autumn soliloquy in Columbia River Basin,
Steamboat Rock State Park

" . . . In the rosy divine glow on the mountains at sunset all the
onlooking landscape seems in sympathy to yield an indefinable subtle
repose."

Douglas fir atop Mount Erie at sunset, looking toward Whidbey Island

Evening's pearly light ascends Heliotrope Ridge,
Mount Baker Wilderness

Overleaf: Evening light flees Lost River Valley past the Bailey Range,
Olympic National Park

"*Over all the other species the Douglas spruce reigns supreme. It is not only a large tree, the tallest in America next to the redwood, but a very beautiful one, with bright green drooping foliage, handsome pendent cones, and a shaft exquisitely straight and round and regular. Forming extensive forests by itself in many places, it lifts its spiky tops into the sky close together with as even a growth as a well-tilled field of grain. . . .*"

Wheat fields ripple down from Steptoe Butte, Whitman County

Dry-land waves, Juniper-Dunes Wilderness

" . . . [The wind] now speeding by on level currents, now whirling in
eddies, or, escaping over the edges of the whirls, soaring aloft on
grand, upswelling domes of air, or tossing on flame-like crests.
Smooth, deep currents, cascades, falls, and swirling eddies, sing
around every tree and leaf, and over all the varied topography of the
region with telling changes of form. . ."

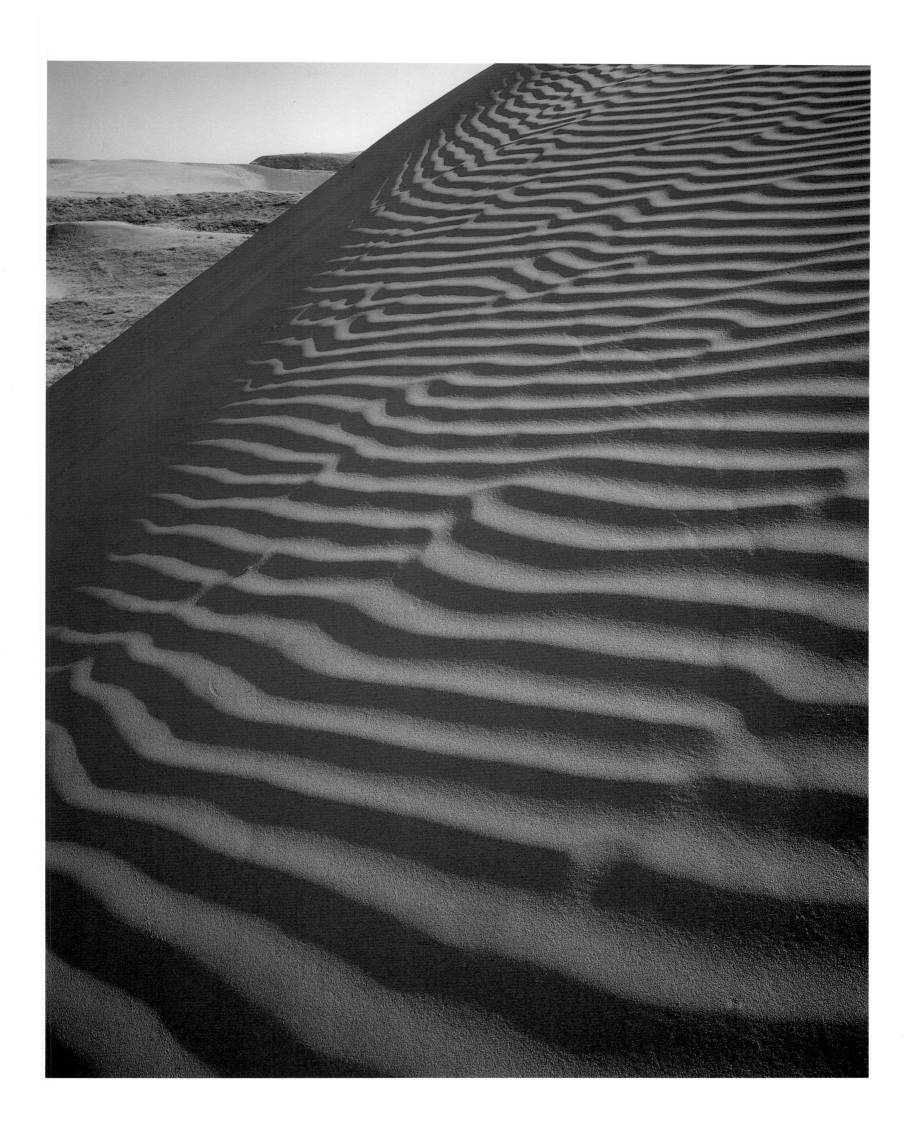

Mount Angeles, Olympic National Park

Blue horizons recede to Cowlitz Towers and Mount Rainier,
Mount Rainier National Park

Overleaf: Evening sweeps across Brush Creek Valley and Mount Shuksan,
North Cascades National Park

"*Out of the forest at last there stood the mountain, wholly unveiled, awful in bulk and majesty, filling all the view like a separate, newborn world, yet withal so fine and beautiful it might well fire the dullest observer to desperate enthusiasm.*"

# TECHNICAL
# INFORMATION

The tools selected to expose most of the images in this book include a Wista 45SP view camera with a variety of Nikkor lenses ranging from 90mm to 360mm and a Nikon F-3 with lenses ranging from 24mm to 300mm. With the exception of aerial photography, all exposures were made with the camera mounted on a sturdy Bogen tripod. A Luna-Pro SBC light meter was used for external readings with the view camera which often resulted in long exposures of ¼ second to 60 seconds. Ektachrome, Fujichrome, and Polaroid Professional Chrome sheet films were selected for view camera exposures while Kodachrome roll films were used with the 35mm gear. Polarizing and 81 Series filters were used occasionally.

### Acknowledgements

I would like to acknowledge the following people for their companionship on backpacking trips and continuous support during the image-making for this book. Tim McNulty, Keith Lazelle, Steve McCurdy, Frank Gilliland, Bill Mitchell, Scott Price, Dave Faith, Dave and Debbie Wukash, Dale Swanson, and Ben Hammond. My appreciation is also extended to Jerry Behrens for keeping me organized in situations of potential chaos. And finally, a loving thanks to Tina for her guiding patience and sensitivity to my vacillating moods.

*Sucia Island at sunset, San Juan Islands*